Designated for Assignment

An Employment Handbook

Richard L. Baran

ISBN: 978-1-7337545-0-7

Table of Contents

Acknowledgements

Thank you to every colleague that I've had the pleasure of spending hours with. Every new industry, position, company, and location has allowed me to learn more about myself. No matter where I've worked throughout my career, two things remain the same: good people are everywhere, and good people attract good people. With every encounter, I continue to learn from each of you.

Special thanks to my dad, Stan, who has been the perennial standard against whom I measure myself and others in the workforce.

Finally, in memory of Jerry York and Terry Wood, two men whose voices I heard often as I worked on this project. Onto the next adventure!

About the Author

Richard Baran holds a JD/MBA from the University of Connecticut and has been employed at organizations ranging in size from startups to large, multinational corporations. His scope of responsibilities to date has spanned from intern to C-suite executive in publicly traded, family-owned, and private equity companies. He has a broad experience base working in both short- and long-cycle businesses in the United States and internationally. Richard also consults with many businesses and investors in their quest to improve operations or assess business development opportunities.

Designated for Assignment

Prologue: Designated for Assignment

For managers, there are countless books and articles about how to lead, how to build an organization, or how to build a business. For employees, there are numerous videos, articles, and social media posts covering countless isolated workplace topics. How-to advice is plentiful, but there are few roadmaps on one most basic need: **how to be a highly valued and sustainable member in your organization and in the workforce**.

When starting a job, particularly at established medium or large firms, employees are often sent to a website or given a manual filled with information on how to obtain benefits, or who to call if certain issues arise. Company credos, soundbites, or an overview of the culture of the business usually fill the remaining pages. But nowhere in these documents will you find the "how to be a successful or great employee" section. Once you make it through the door, it is assumed you will be great in your role, figuring out the rest as you go.

This handbook is an attempt to provide some supplemental navigation skills for any employee, from entry-level intern to the C-suite executive. These thoughts represent decades of collective learning gained from a slew of observations and conversations with everyone from janitorial staff to CEOs. Ideally, you and your employer share the goal of long-term mutual success. But even if you have been hired for just the summer or are simply earning some extra cash in your free time, the purpose of this guide is to provide you with insights and perhaps a little secret sauce for success.

Chapter 1: The Must-Have Attributes

When you strip away the specialized skills or behaviors required for a role, there are in the end only six attributes everyone must have, regardless of the job. Every successful employee with staying power possesses *all* of them. Put another way, if you are missing even one of these on a consistent basis, you will probably not remain in your role for very long. These must-have attributes are not ranked in any order of importance, as they are all critical.

Competence

Delusions are possible about many things: how you believe people view you, how you view others or situations, even your runway to future career success. But it is nearly impossible to be delusional about your competence. Once you have been performing a job, task, or game for any period of time, you can quickly figure out exactly where you fit in the scheme of things.

Let's take a sports example. In baseball, you can either hit a curve ball or you can't. You can throw a 90-mph fastball or you can't. You can field a 110-mph short hop ground ball or you can't. Even if most of us were to train and practice eighteen hours a day, we would never be able to perform at a major league level. Even athletes who *can* do one or more of these things realize their limitations in other areas of their game.

The first requirement of any worker is to match your ability to the role you will play. Most job requirements have obvious ways of determining someone's ability. If, for example, you can't make change in your head, being a cashier may not be a position in which you will succeed. Many roles however, have less visible but just as vital competencies, and any deficiencies can and will be exposed over time.

It is possible and actually pretty common to find yourself initially mismatched for a role. You may be asked to do something you cannot. Most positions have some duties that play to your strengths and others you'll find more difficult. You can probably think of people you know who are not well suited for their job. In most cases, within a short period of time, the employee will be the first one to realize that one or more required skills are just not in their toolkit. Your management will ultimately discover it as well.

Maybe you got lucky or bluffed your way into a position knowing you did not have one or more of the required skills and hoping to pick it up on the job. Make no mistake, even casual sports fans quickly notice player shortcomings. Eventually, people *will* recognize discrepancies between the job expectations and your performance. In every job, you must take responsibility for your competence level and strive for constant improvement.

We all have areas where we need to grow and improve, so don't ever let fear delude you into thinking you can't do it. Doubt is the precursor of fear, and many careers have hit roadblocks only because people didn't believe they could accomplish a task and subsequently didn't even try. You were hired because the organization (or at least your hiring manager) believes in your ability to do it.

A great reminder for me of overcoming the fear of competence happened at a water park when my son was eight years old. He was eager to try the highest slide, and (on paper) the requirements seemed easy: be at least a certain height, know how to swim, get up the slide, come down. Still, as we climbed the stairs in line, he became paralyzed with fear. When we finally arrived at the top, with only a couple of riders ahead of us, he said, "I don't want to do it anymore. Let's go."

Since I wasn't too crazy myself about following him down, I said "Are you sure? It's your call." As we began our walk of shame back down the stairs, a determined look came over his face, one I have seen more than a few times since on many different faces. By the time we had returned to the end of the line, he turned around and said, "Dad, I'm sorry, but I'm doing this."

We got back in line. After another slow climb, we returned to the top. His legs were shaking. The last thing he wanted to do was get into that tube. But not going down this time was not an option. Off he went, into the darkness by himself. I worried about what I would find when I reached the pool below a minute later, but when we reunited, his enormous smile flashed a combination of relief and accomplishment. It was a classic father-son moment. "Want to go again?" I asked. He replied, "No, I'm good." What mattered was that now *he knew he could do it*. He had made a literal leap of faith to prove it to himself. He was now a competent water slide rider, even if he never chose to do it again.

Your job will require different core competencies. Some may be intangible, like business judgement, communication skills, or resourcefulness. It is critical that you understand all job aspects, but moreover that you discern the nuances of competence required. Even if you receive training materials, ultimately only *you* can accept responsibility and exercise personal discipline to gain all of the required skills and continue to build them.

As my son proved, simply having the ability to do a job is not competence. Possessing skill or potential (height, ability to swim, etc.) is not competence. **Competence is a**

combination of ability to execute and actually performing well and on time. Once trained, your ability to execute, time after time, is mandatory.

Adaptability

"Adapt or die." -Brad Pitt as Billy Beane in *Moneyball*

As in personal relationships, your work relationship should ideally be sustained, mutual beneficial, and open to adaptation. If you can't or won't adapt to changes in the company, your manager, or your role, people will notice quickly. Today, business transformation happens at an ever-increasing rate. As an employee, recognizing and embracing change as the norm is vital to maintaining your position now and in the future.

I was having lunch with the CEO of a popular online dating service when he asked me what I thought the was the key to a lasting marriage—in one word. Having been married for several decades, I thought for a second, and rattled off words like *love, compatibility, honesty* and *trust*.

My CEO friend shook his head and said, "I have been doing this for a very long time, and the only answer is *adaptability*. Over time, almost every variable will change in a relationship—economics, age, growth, hardship, goals. Unless both people are committed to adapting to the changes in themselves and their partner, the relationship won't last."

The same wisdom is true in every business relationship. Unless you can adapt to changing circumstances and initiatives, you won't last long in any organization. Likely, the business will look very different in a year or two. You may have a new boss, the products or services may change, or the company may undergo exponential growth. Or retraction. The daily news gives many examples of how scandal or good fortune requires companies to pivot quickly.

Your firm will make some decisions you disagree with. If you truly believe a certain move or change can be done better, or perhaps is not in the organization's best interests, you have an obligation to speak up. If, after voicing your objective concerns, the organization still proceeds, your job is to adapt to these moves. Failing to adapt or resisting change ultimately only delay the inevitable: you won't last in the job. Passive aggressive resistance or direct challenges to what you might view as bad decisions are a waste of your time and energy. As long as the initiatives or changes do not involve illegal or unethical behavior, your adaptability, support, and even leadership in the transformation is expected. As long as you are never asked to sacrifice your personal integrity, you need to embrace change, despite any personal or even potentially negative impact on you or your coworkers.

I have had many moments throughout my career when I was challenged to adapt or decide whether to take a stand. Once, I was actually asked to look the other way as an executive tried to make a sizable donation in a fashion that it would not be detected by investors or the board of directors. The CEO above this executive had told him it would be ok and that it had been done before, but the employee manual and delegation of authority guidelines said otherwise. My internal compass told me that this decision was wrong, and that I could not endorse a culture of doing one thing while saying another. I spoke out against the decision and even took my concerns to members of the board. Unfortunately, the response was "technically, you are right, but we're ok letting it slide." Everyone knew these actions could get others fired, but the executives in the C-suite were somehow exempt. Clear rules became suggestions that could be ignored, and the leadership expected me to simply adapt to this "new normal." After much thought, I knew I could not do what they were asking. My personal ethics were at stake, so I came to the conclusion that I needed to start looking for a new job.

While this is an example of an ethical line crossed, you undoubtedly will encounter less obvious situations with various shades of gray. It is a good practice to be aware of both the overt and subtle changes around you at work so you can decide whether to adapt or take a personal stand.

Executes Through Adversity

"The ultimate measure of a man is not where he stands in moments of comfort and convenience, but where he stands at times of challenge and controversy." -Martin Luther King Jr.

How do you respond under stress? Colleagues and supervisors will quickly discover the answer, so self-awareness is vital. It's always good to know your own tendencies, actions, and reactions—a bit like knowing whether alcohol makes you angry, passive, silly, affectionate, etc. If pressure brings out your negative personality traits or inhibits your performance, you need to dedicate yourself to changing these behaviors.

When the heat gets turned up, you need to rise to the challenge. Many people can cope with a changing environment, but don't perform well with tight deadlines, high pressure, conflict, or crisis. When a disaster strikes or stakes rise, do you act like a first responder and run toward solving the problem? Or do you have a flight response that sends you searching for an exit? Do your emotions cause you to act out? Employers value those who perform well under pressure. They need people who are *comfortable being uncomfortable*. Employees are expected to be able to answer the bell. Every time.

After a successful tournament in the 1980s, PGA golfer Fuzzy Zoeller was asked about handling adversity. His response illustrates what I mean by getting comfortable being uncomfortable: "The golf course is my office. The pressure and excitement keep me coming back. I never really get tense. I try to leave that in the hotel room. I'm not afraid to choke, if that's what you call it. In fact, I always want to be in position to choke."

I recall a takeoff during stormy weather, just as the flight attendants were unbuckling their belts to prepare for drink service. Suddenly, there was a very loud bang and flash of light, and a strange orange glow outside the windows. My first thought was that the plane had hit something, and I was feeling anything but calm. Worse, both flight attendants in front of me grabbed onto the walls, their eyes wide with fear. One of them quickly called the cockpit and yelled, "What happened?" into the phone.

As you can imagine, the flight attendants' reactions made the rest of us even more nervous. After what seemed like an eternity, the flight attendant hung up and shakily whispered to her colleague but was looking a bit calmer. The pilot then announced that lightening had struck the plane, but everything was operating normally. Then, he apologized for the behavior of the flight attendants. "They haven't been through that before," he joked. Now that they'd learned what a lightning strike felt like, the pilot promised, they would react better the next time it happened.

The passengers were not happy. Many voiced their dissatisfaction with the crew or said they would never fly this airline again because of the unprofessional conduct during a moment of uncertainty. By the time the plane landed, both attendants were very worried about their jobs. They had not performed well under pressure, and they knew it.

The course of a career can best be defined as a series of comebacks, not only from the failures but from the successes as well. Every role has a shelf life, which is to say that none of them lasts forever. Along the way you will experience adversity (or turbulence). How you respond and persevere is what matters. Every day, you need to show your company that you are steady and reliable, regardless of what distractions, ambiguities, or added pressures arise.

Work Ethic

No one is likely to admit to having a bad work ethic, but the old adage, "20 percent of the people do 80 percent of the work," has staying power for a reason. Role models for a good work ethic abound. Family members, entrepreneurs, and coworkers can all be sources of inspiration. Of course, it's not just the time someone commits to a task, but the willingness to go the extra mile, regardless of the roadblocks to success. One of my previous bosses called it the "willing to eat tree bark" characteristic. He explained, "If I ask someone on the team to do something difficult, I can tell who is willing to eat tree bark if that's what is required to get it done." There has to be a zealous desire to complete the job, with procrastination never being an option.

Employees with a great work ethic see their jobs not as work, but as an extension of their lifestyle. It's part of their DNA to clock in first and clock out last. If someone is needed to go into the plant at 3:00 a.m. to fix something or perform an inventory count, they are the first to volunteer. They are the players who are in the gym at 5:00 a.m. working on their game. They relish the challenge to complete tasks and stay on top of their productivity. Work ethic is not the same as competence. There are many employees who may be able to simply do the job, but work ethic is like a steroid that boosts performance beyond normal expectations.

If you don't give maximum effort every day, you need to ask yourself why. The truth might be that your role doesn't call for it. Or maybe, over time, you have developed short cuts or technical advances that make your job easier. A good analogy is running a race. The job is to complete the course. Everyone might finish the race, but it is easy to see who has the real work ethic. They are the ones always trying to beat their personal best times, always pushing to increase their speed and endurance. They can be found in the winner's circle *and* at the back of the pack. They don't always outperform everyone else, but they are the ones pushing themselves to their limit the whole way.

In a race, you will also notice the folks who are just out for fun, or to collect a participation medal or free t-shirt. They will finish the race, but their bodies have adjusted to the pace they have set for themselves, which is another way of saying the status quo. These runners are not out to improve. You should, at all costs, avoid this trap of coasting for a paycheck, of being satisfied with just getting by. Over time, your company will spot mediocrity and weed it out. Leaders know who's creating bandwidth and who's using it up. Football coach Vince Lombardi said it best: "If you aren't fired with enthusiasm, you'll get fired with enthusiasm."

Employees with a strong work ethic put in all the blood, sweat, and tears necessary, but it is the satisfaction of a job well done that drives them. They are not necessarily seeking tangible rewards. The back of the pack runner who sets a personal best time is often the happiest person you will find at the finish line. Their effort is inspirational. Employees with a strong work ethic are never satisfied with being "just ok."

One summer, I worked on a landscaping and tree removal crew for the highway department. I remember some guys being angry with those of us who went all-out every day to complete the work. "Slow down! You're making the rest of us look bad," was their repeated messaging to us. They resented and often belittled the hardest-working guys, trying to get us to play down to their level. Thankfully, this strategy failed, since people who work hard find it impossible to diminish their effort level. Not performing at their best is never an option. Ultimately, they make the other folks on the team *better* by their example, which is exactly what happened to that summer team, and to many others since.

Fit

A great white shark may have a fantastic resume filled with successful seal hunts, but it would never mesh well with a pod of killer whales who do the same. Similarly, an introvert will not succeed in a company with a gregarious people-person culture. Frankly, you can be outstanding in every other attribute, but if you are water in a company of oil, it will never work. If your personality or values don't mesh with the business, your career may be limited. Always remember: companies hire and retain who they *want*, not necessarily who they *need*. Lack of compatibility will cause tension and unproductive energy among teams. Even Steve Jobs, the founder of Apple, was once asked to leave his business due to a problem of fit. Despite skill or passion, ultimately other people's assessment of your fit can determine whether you stay or go. You are supplying skills to your job, but your company is always evaluating its demand for those skills or any perceived excess baggage you may be carrying.

Even intangibles like "perceived loyalty" are important fit factors for many companies. You may be the perfect employee in every other way, but if management believes you have your sights set on another position, are a "flight risk," or won't take direction well, you may be asked to depart.

Fit is the primary reason companies use "employment at will" language. All else being equal, it is very difficult to terminate someone who is doing their job well. It is critical that you identify any gaps between your personal style or beliefs and your supervisor's or the company's. Know how you mesh and know how that might change over time. Like every part of life, some degree of conformity and compromise is necessary.

A former coworker of mine never clearly understood how his team or management viewed him. He believed others saw him as a change agent and a vocal leader. But the entire team actually viewed him as a malcontent. He was shocked when the business asked him to pack up his belongings and leave the company.

Integrity

I once worked with a financial controller who kept books for a multi-billion-dollar firm yet completely lacked personal integrity. On the golf course, he would shamelessly cheat on his scorecard. On business trips, he covertly visited strip clubs at the company's expense, yet he expounded fiduciary duties and strict cost control in team meetings.

Your integrity is at the core of who you are, and during your career it can be your greatest asset or your undoing. In truth, you may experience work situations that conflict with your values. You may even be tempted to rationalize a departure from your personal integrity on the job. *Never do that.*

Your truthfulness, confidentiality, accountability, and trustworthiness are components of your integrity. Ensure that in all of your actions and words, you can pass the courtroom or newspaper tests. In other words, if something you say or do on the job were to be presented in court or appear in print, be sure you would proudly stand behind it.

Do you know where you draw the line when it comes to your integrity? Does that line match your company's? In the event of a conflict, could you literally put your job on the line to do the right thing? If your company culture plays in ethical gray areas, are you doing anything to change it? Is it even possible for you to influence your work environment? These are critical questions to ask yourself regardless of your position.

In a prior corporate role, I was tasked with minimizing expenses over a short period of time. Every Wednesday, a friendly long-term vendor named Linda wandered through our building. Everyone knew and liked her. She was attractive and had a great personality. It was rumored she had once dated one of the company's founders. She was also the office "plant lady," who would provide and care for plants to the office, for everyone from secretaries to the CEO. Her services were nominal given the size of the business, however the company was on the verge of bankruptcy and needed to reduce costs. Not to mention the optics of a weekly plant service were bad.

One day, Linda arrived unsolicited with a large plant for me that cost over $1,000, along with similarly priced ones for dozens of other employees. I told her I did not want the plant, and to return it. The next day, I found the plant in one of my direct report's offices. Apparently, the CEO had suggested the plant lady leave it there instead. I met said to the CEO later that day and said, "It's hard for me to move the needle on costs when we allow practices like this to continue." The CEO responded, "Look, things are not going well, but if we go under it won't be the plant expense that does it. If you don't want your employee to get the plant, just tell Linda to give it to someone else."

My lesson was that the CEO valued his weekly interactions with Linda more than stewardship of the company assets. While I lost this battle, my personal integrity remained intact, and I believed I had done the right thing by speaking out. Still, it is problematic when your personal level of integrity differs from that of your company, especially when that disparity prevents you from completing stated objectives. On the job, are you surrounded by one or more people who will speak up and ask for accountability if asked to do something unethical or even illegal? Are you that person?

A former colleague who had once worked at the White House passed onto me the advice he received when he first started working for a former President. "One day, you will leave here on your own accord or at the request of the President. Regardless of which, make sure that when that day comes you can look yourself in the mirror knowing you did your absolute best for the country and that you maintained your personal integrity every day."

Even if you have been with your business for decades, remember that one day the relationship will end. Performing your job with integrity and leaving the role as a trusted steward of the organization should be your legacy.

Your Six Tools

In reality, having all six tools in your toolbox doesn't guarantee employment. Indeed, there are many roles, particularly in the short term, that never require you to work through adversity, adapt to a changing culture, or demonstrate a peerless work ethic. Great employees still get laid off when plants close, or a business goes under. Absent those circumstances, knowing who has all six must-have attributes will determine how companies make difficult decisions. If a company experiences a downsizing, the employees with every tool have the best chances of being retained. And even if bad things happen to good people (as they sometimes do), the attributes give you the greatest chances for future employment.

It's a smart move to regularly review how well you have developed these attributes, and how well people at your company recognize them in you. Asking colleagues for objective feedback can be uncomfortable but will be well worth the effort. It's ultimately up to you to cultivate and hone your tools, and constantly seek to improve yourself.

Chapter 2: What Your Company Does (For Now)

Let's dig a little deeper into the idea of fit. Every employee, regardless of rank or status, should understand the company's mission and core values, along with where they fit within the company. This includes knowing the macro goals, challenges, and current performance of the business. Across jobs in all kinds of organizations, my biggest frustration has been how few people really understand the bigger picture of where they fit into the overall structure, or even what their coworkers do. Many employees are content to perform their assigned tasks, keep a low profile, and leave the building as soon as business hours end.

Occasionally, I begin meetings by asking employees a few softball questions in exchange for a small prize. Things like, "What was the revenue for this company last quarter?" or "Who is our largest customer?" or "What was our cash flow last quarter?" At first, my questions are met with awkward silence or worse, answers that are way off.

People grow very comfortable focusing on their isolated tasks without looking around to see what else is going on in the business, which holds them back in the long run from ever developing the six attributes covered in Chapter 1. The good news is, over time, the teams I questioned learned to prepare and build their company knowledge. Truly, what gets measured gets accomplished.

Regardless of your role in any organization, you need to understand why it started in the first place. Your job fits somewhere in the puzzle of the company's product or service, customers, and larger purpose. If you don't see the connection among all these aspects, you are in trouble. These are the vital organs of the business, and in down cycles or expense reductions, the vital workers are the ones who keep these organs functioning.

It is a good habit to ask yourself regularly, "Why am I working here?" Maybe the answer is obvious—you're working for the only steady employer in your area or hold one of the few positions available in your field. Even so, over time your job satisfaction can diminish, and an honest answer about why you are there is critical.

We tend to think very large companies are unlikely to change over time, but General Electric (GE) is an example of how quickly things can shift. Thirty years ago, GE was a renowned leader across most markets, always making the list of most admired companies. Winning in the marketplace was its highest priority. Employees knew the company was financially focused, with meticulous attention paid to all operational details and accurate projections of results. GE was a strong brand, with various units performing together like a finely tuned orchestra, year after year. And it was a magnet for talented people, the envy of the corporate world with a highly-regarded culture of meritocracy and a deep bench of managers. There was a rigorous annual performance evaluation process for all employees, often with a "rank and yank" result.

Over time, however, this culture changed. Meritocracy was supplanted with criteria like being a master black belt in Six Sigma methodology. The company became more recognized for promoting work-life balance, being a good neighbor in cities where they operated, and shifting from a financial to a marketing focus. None of these changes are inherently problematic; taken in isolation, any of them could have been net positives. But when the Great Recession hit in 2008, financial targets were missed, and the brand grew stale. An increasing focus on its financial services businesses suddenly became a bad bet. Today, the brand resorts to marketing itself on NBA uniforms in an attempt to stay relevant. The company is almost unrecognizable from its former self after many sea change decisions. They stopped doing annual performance reviews altogether, for example. Focus shifted to "outcomes," not "performance." New skills were required of employees, and intangibles like "mindfulness" became important.

Large enterprises like GE usually take longer to change their culture, but it can happen instantaneously in response to a shock to the system—scandal, corruption, a major divestiture, or acquisition can change the status quo literally overnight. So, make sure you stay aware of any changing winds in the company's performance or priorities. Just like the crew of a ship, you need to know where the vessel is heading, track any change in course, and know whether it is anchored or adrift.

At GE, one can see in hindsight the decisions that steered its gradual transformation. Departments like Human Resources and Finance—key components providing vital checks and balances—subtly shifted focus to other activities. In essence, many procedures that were once key differentiators began to look and feel the same as most other companies, as with employee reviews. Even minor management process changes in areas like capital allocation, internal audits, and business development criteria can contribute to an unintended cultural transformation.

Make a point to study the Key Performance Indicators (KPIs) of your company. These are critical metrics that leadership looks at regularly. Understand why those particular metrics have been chosen and which get added to or removed from the tracking dashboard over time.

Certain metrics can indicate when problems may be surfacing. Ask yourself if your job is vital to those metrics improving. Again, successful employees understand the business model and how they fit into it. If you don't know the KPIs your company tracks, find people who can tell you. Don't be part of the crowd that simply wonders what is happening.

Here are some other key questions to ask yourself: Do you understand the company's culture and the priorities of the management power base? Does management walk the walk or are there conflicting objectives in place? Do the various functions (operations, sales, HR, legal, etc.) all row in the same direction, or do political or relationship barriers prevent that? Are one or more functions viewed as more important or have more clout than others?

If you are at a startup, especially in the very early days, the entire team must be aware of everything. One of the great advantages of very small companies is allowing employees access to everything going on. There simply isn't time or resources available to afford anything less.

Regardless of the size or maturity of your organization, make yourself aware of whether your business is generating cash or burning it off each quarter. Cash flow is oxygen to a business, and new companies in particular need it along with little luck if they hope to get to maturity. If your business is losing cash consistently quarter after quarter, make sure you know the plan to turn the tide. If it is sustainably spinning off cash, you should be aware of how that asset is being utilized.

Chapter 3: Tangibles and Intangibles

One of my colleagues was recently recognized with a significant management award, and she graciously accepted it by giving credit to the entire team. She felt embarrassed by the attention and in fact cut the ceremony short to get back to work without basking in the moment. Later in the day, someone approached her, "You didn't even stay for the cake or the recognition that were really well deserved. Is everything ok?" My friend just smiled and said, "My dad told me long ago how things work in business. One day you will be considered an ace and the next day you be considered an ass. Just stay focused on doing your job to the best of your ability."

Understanding and quickly excelling at the rules of engagement will play a huge part in present and future opportunities. Like my coworker, your ability to remain level-headed and focused on your job responsibilities will determine your future success. Those job responsibilities require continuous adjustment on your part, and an understanding of some of the intangibles that may affect them.

Get Quick Wins

Every job comes with at least a basic description of duties and tasks you must handle. Never assume these general tasks are the only aspects of your job. At best, they are a starting point, the lowest expectations, and likely what the previous person in your role did. Either way, you'll want to set yourself apart and go beyond just the minimum.

In reality, your job description might differ from what your company actually *wants* you to do. For example, a job description will never ask for merely status quo performance, but unfortunately in the short term, that may be all the company asks of you. For example, you may want to change a process to save time or money but be aware of whether your supervisor prefers the approach of "if it ain't broke, don't fix it." Work through this noise when you can and keep focused on playing offense.

Regardless of how long you have been in your role, identify at least two additional achievements or initiatives for yourself over the next ninety days. Also, come up with two longer-term aspirational goals for the next six to twelve months. They can be personal improvement goals (a class at a local university, joining a networking group in your field, etc.) or additional responsibilities that increase your value to the company. Assess your progress and update your goals as you go. Remember, you will miss 100 percent of the shots you never take. Imagine what successes or wins you want to be able to boast about during your performance review a year from now. Just being able to say "I did what I was told" should never suffice.

Seek Work, Not a Title

Have you noticed the trend of giving out titles like "executive" to analysts and "Vice President" to managers? Sales people are now "account executives" and sourcing managers have morphed into Chief Procurement Officers. We have oversold jobs and become infatuated with empty titles. For example, by definition there can be only one chief financial officer at any company—the person who signs off on the financials, attests to their accuracy, and oversees the financial controls. However, at a past firm, there were five individuals who carried the title CFO—one real one and four others who just enjoyed the title on their business cards.

Beware of taking a role just to get a meaningless title. Thousands of people on Wall Street carry the seemingly lowly title of Analyst yet earn seven-figure salaries. In many companies, the best sales people often make twice as much as those with the sexy job names. You need to seek out job *responsibilities* and the rewards for executing them, rather than grab a watered-down title with less impact.

Ultimately, most businesses are organized like a bee hive. There is one queen: The Board and CEO. Everyone else is a worker. As such, your title is somewhat irrelevant, since you serve at the pleasure of the queen. Even those with C-suite titles are ultimately are there for the same reason—they just have more access, power and resources.

Manage Expectations

I was headed to the airport, satisfied after spending six weeks on completing a Long-Range Forecast (LRF). Then my boss called. "The LRF has been changed by CEO. Everything went up by 3-5%. I will send you the new numbers." Keep in mind that books had already been printed for a presentation to the Board of Directors, with our lock-solid, data-driven forecast from extensive research and analytics. My boss stayed quiet as I ranted about deviating from reality, then finally said, "I agree with you, but he wants to show the board a brighter outlook."

I felt compelled to let those receiving the "revised" estimates know that they were not supported by data. I felt a responsibility to manage expectations based on integrity and stewardship, so this revision request felt counter to my very DNA. But my boss had made his decision. As you might have guessed, the additional 3-5% never panned out, but during his presentation, that CEO was applauded for his bright outlook.

Maintaining a realistic view of the landscape is at the core of your job duties, as is communicating that realistic outlook. Your credibility with the organization depends on it. If you are not successful at actively managing expectations, both short- and longer-term, you will be at the mercy of often unrealistic expectations set by others.

Politics

The larger the company, the more political forces will impact all aspects of the business. Your task is to discover the real path or "true north" of your employer. For your job, you might already be aware that there is often a difference between a stated objective and the real one. You could be asked to reduce headcount by 10 percent across the board yet be told behind closed doors which groups are not to be touched. You may be asked to reduce costs by 5 percent, but not those that would upset special constituencies (i.e., the plant lady).

Many other examples abound. A company may have a rigorous sourcing procedure requiring multiple bids, but you may have to privilege the known favorite suppliers of the board of directors. There may be a mandate to quickly optimize processes or operations, but with the actual requirement to go very slowly to avoid discomfort. Political forces are always in play. Sometimes there are fall guys or collateral damage that result. Understanding who holds the real power and (more importantly) understanding what they *really* want is vital. You find clues by looking at how the company allocates its capital expenses. Most firms will put money into their real priorities, whether or not they are stated.

If money isn't a factor, there is often an art to differentiating stated objectives from true intentions. The Six Sigma initiative that Jack Welch launched decades ago at GE is a great example. Sometimes, leaders take extreme positions or set unreachable goals, simply to move the needle a little bit. Welch made bold mandates like, "We will be a Six Sigma company within five years" and "Anyone who does not have a master black belt certification will not be promoted to senior levels." These and other mandates caused significant angst among the rank and file.

But Welch understood that if a company with revenue of $100 billion was going to improve quality and efficiency, these positions were necessary. Every employee understood that they needed to get onboard for the good of the company and their personal careers. So, while the company did not—and could not—achieve 99.9 percent efficiency and quality, it did gain significant improvements in a short period of time. The best employees heard the real message: quality improvement with rigorous tools is the new priority. Those who focused on only the *stated* goals were left bewildered and frustrated.

On a macro scale, you often see this tactic used with issues like national security (build a 2,000-mile wall!), national health care (without Obamacare, millions will die!), or national finances (without Brexit, the UK economy will collapse!). Employees need to differentiate stated goals from attempts to exert influence or drive change in a particular direction.

Innovation

Regardless of political or other pressures, as a general premise, companies value innovation. On a macro level, that simply means improving the business—either making the product or service better or more efficient, reducing cost or time, or improving customer service. In any particular role, it means finding ways to increase productivity with better and faster methods. It is highly unlikely that your company will want you to simply maintain your current performance with no improvements in sight—the "I did what I was told" approach. Ask yourself if you are bringing innovation to your role or to the team.

The basic ingredients for innovation are work ethic, imagination, and the refusal to accept failure. Whether you innovate by doing something new or borrowing ideas from others, what will matter is your ability to consistently seek positive disruption of the status quo.

Communication

Every single communication falls into one of three categories: information, noise, or redundancy. Strive to remove all the noise and redundancy from your business communications, and always aim for clarity, concision, and persuasion. Use "we" instead of "I" as often as you can to demonstrate focus on the entire team whenever you can. I often tell my teams to be French not Scottish, i.e., say *oui* instead of *aye*.

Bad communication only loses you time, energy, trust, and respect. I recall an incident when the leadership team of my large firm was called into a conference room. Our president gave the team a task: come up with the top five problems in our company and create initiatives with deadlines to solve them. Over the next four hours, the team covered the walls with large sheets of paper outlining problems and assigning team members to solve them. At lunch, the president returned for a session review of the issues and our plans. After hearing us all out, he said, "Nice ideas, but here is what we are going to do." He proceeded to hand out a list of initiatives he had already come up with on his own days earlier. Only one of his matched ours, and none of the teams he formed aligned with our abilities. As you can imagine, this broke everyone's spirit. There could be no pushback—the president had spoken and his (unstated) message was clear: he would do things his way, he was immune to changing course, and communication went in only one direction. Unsurprisingly, over the next three months, little was accomplished. We made presentation decks and held many report outs, but no tangible results were ever achieved.

Learn the difficult art of saying the right thing at the right time. Anyone can blurt out something that may be 100 percent correct, but which, if said at the wrong time or in the wrong forum, can totally negate the message. Similarly, remaining silent when clear and concise communication is called for will send an unintended message. If you are frustrated by a consistent inability to communicate effectively, seek resources to help you work on this skill. Many people can spew rhetoric- aspire to be one of the few who communicates effectively.

Keep It Professional

It is now a very fine line between a flattering comment and a remark that is perceived as harassment. Don't ever assume how something you say will be interpreted by anyone, regardless of how long you have been colleagues or how well you know someone. Even when attending functions after hours, respect and professionalism for your coworkers is of utmost importance.

You may think you are hilarious but remember not everyone will think so. Avoid being the person who gives nicknames to coworkers or management, for example. Don't use your workspace to make a visual statement about your personal, political, or religious views. You can't assume that your colleagues will want to support your child's fundraising activities, unless you are willing to support every one of theirs. Your company's culture usually will give clear direction on what is considered appropriate. Follow that direction.

Chapter 4: How People See You

Despite the diversity you will encounter at work, there are actually only five ways that we all view each other. These perceptions impact our relationships, trust, and daily interactions.

The Indifferent

The opposite of love is not hate. It is indifference. In any company, particularly a larger one, many—if not most—of your colleagues don't care that much about you. The people we pass in the halls or hold the elevator for are usually completely indifferent to us. Recognizing this fact should be easy, but somehow our ego makes us forget and take things personally. Understanding that in business, most of what you bring is replaceable and you don't occupy most people's minds for very long, is valuable knowledge.

In a prior life, I worked for a large conglomerate with hundreds of thousands of employees, and regularly attended large town hall style employee gatherings. At one of these, the head of Human Resources was asked about recent attrition rates, and monotoned that over the past decade, there were only "a handful" of truly regrettable losses among the thousands of departed colleagues. At the reception that followed, this comment really bothered some attendees, who expressed anger about the firm's indifference to their colleagues' departures. But the rest of us were simply reminded that as long as operations continue to grow and prosper, the company was and would remain indifferent to any particular employee's exit.

The challenge for us as individuals is to not mentally move the people we engage with professionally to our indifferent list. No one enjoys being ignored or being viewed indifferently, even if it is common and to be expected. To the greatest extent possible, make an effort to know your colleagues well enough to form an objective opinion about them. When people are indifferent about you and your work, you'll miss out on valuable feedback, both positive and negative.

The Disinclined

We all have people we dislike and don't look forward to interacting with, whether because of differing styles, personalities, habits, approaches, or values. As individuals, we naturally seek out symbiotic energy and avoid conflict. In business, this human diversity is not only normal but can be quite valuable, a fact that has been well documented. Everyone brings something unique to the ecosystem. It is important to recognize when differences can become problematic and monitor those possibilities.

I can recall an instance of a job opening that wasn't getting filled, due to the hiring manager's well-deserved bad reputation. This person was known for her lack of flexibility and was not well respected. She did not get along with most of her subordinates and sometimes passed judgment on their car or clothes. But because of her connections and valuable skillset, she had remained in the job for an extremely long time, despite her flaws.

I decided to take the open position at the request of my supervisor at the time, knowing that our personalities were a bad fit. It was hoped that I could be the one to make a difficult dynamic work. While I filled a short-term need for the business, and appreciated the new salary and location, in the end, it's rarely a good idea to put yourself in a situation with this much potential for conflict. My very first day on the job, she insulted my car choice and told me to buy another one "if you expect to work for me." Unsurprisingly, the relationship lasted less than a year, and we couldn't wait to get away from each other.

It's hard to change your opinion about someone without actively trying to free yourself from old perceptions. With time and effort, it's possible to change our negative stance on someone, but most of the time we tend to stick with our initial assessments, especially after we have shared them openly with others in the hallway.

Here's one example of moving the needle a bit. A former boss had an aversion to me from the first interview, and I knew it. All of his questions were either accusatory or dismissive, so much so that it was hard to ignore the "we are not going to work well together" vibe. He was dissatisfied with all my responses and randomly questioned my mental toughness. I still got the job, and over a period of about six months, he began to see things about me he valued, and more importantly he was getting positive feedback about me from team members he respected. Over dinner about a year later he said, "When I first interviewed you, I wasn't high on you at all. But the relationship has been straight up from there." Turns out, his boss had been convinced that I was right for the role, so he dutifully but reluctantly went along. This person ended up being a mentor and one of my biggest supporters. Strange as it may seem, I think our rough start made the relationship even better in the end.

Discovering your disinclined coworkers is often very hard because they usually only expose their opinions when you are not around. People rarely seek out opportunities to tell someone, "This is what I don't like about you," and even more rarely try to confront their dislike and do something about it. Often, instead of refreshing candor, disinclination will surface in other ways. A manager might create a false narrative about work performance, which is easier than saying there is a "fit" problem, or that you just don't like each other. It takes a lot of effort and a level of shared respect to fix a difficult relationship.

It's easy to say why we don't like certain people, but much harder to see why we could be on other people's lists. It often comes as a surprise if we don't occasionally practice honest self-reflection. I recall one incident when a colleague discovered this in an unexpected way. He and I joined a conference call a few minutes into the conversation and muted our end to listen to the updates from the group. Unaware that we were on the line, someone on the other end made disparaging remarks about my colleague, taking us both by surprise. Understandably, he was mortified, and immediately reached out to the person to try to build a better relationship.

Unfortunately, colleagues can act out their feelings with their jobs or their influence over your position. An IT person may take forever to order a new computer for someone they dislike while helping someone viewed favorably within hours. An HR recruiter may purposefully slow roll a job opening because they dislike the hiring manager. A sales person may resist calling on a client until the last possible moment because their personalities clash. I'm sure you have your own examples to add. For obvious reasons, you need to be vigilant against letting your personal feelings impact your professionalism. In the end, pettiness causes loss of productivity. We all have personal biases. Just make sure you are not wasting effort or energy on negativity.

The Fans

Fans are those people who know you, but like you anyway. They may not even really know you, but for whatever reason, they just are wired to admire you or develop an affinity for your personality, results, or approach. When there are group projects, they want to be on your team. They may even want to hang out after work. When someone asks your fans about you, they respond, "I really like how she gets things done," or "I think he is going places." For people we like, we serve as glowing references, offer our assistance, and prioritize their needs.

You might not be fortunate enough to know who your fans are until after you have left a position, or until the chips are down. Like a loyal sports fan, yours will wear your colors and have your back. False and fair-weather fans will quickly grow indifferent or worse once you leave.

Sometimes, people become fans for the most unexpected reasons. Once, I drove my manager to the airport. I moved the stuff in my trunk to make room for his luggage and noticed his demeanor changed after that one moment. After returning from the trip, our interactions all grew extremely positive. I asked him why our relationship had improved so dramatically in such a short period of time. His response taught me a lot about how fans are made. "I noticed in your trunk that you had your fishing poles and golf clubs. It looked just like my trunk! Anyone who travels with their fishing gear in their car is my kind of person." Without really doing anything, I had gained a fan. I also realized that if he had seen something in my trunk he was opposed to, the outcome could have been completely different.

Obviously, you want your fanbase to grow as large as possible. In business, the more fans you can develop, particularly higher up on the organization chart, the more secure your position. Your access to capital, promotions, and general wellbeing are greatly enhanced with fans higher up in the food chain or directly linked to your advancement opportunities. Similarly, people below are more likely to seek your guidance on issues and problems if they like and respect you. They may also give you a heads-up if they hear negative comments about you. Building a following is one of the best ways to ensure long-term job satisfaction, security and heightened performance. Build the largest following you can in every job.

The Mentors

Mentors are rare and powerful forces in your professional or personal life. Until you have one, you can't really understand the benefits. The mentor goes far beyond fan status, and true mentors stay with you for life. Mentors can't be artificially created or forced. Companies often create mentoring programs that put people together for a lunch a few times a year, but these rarely ever blossom into true mentor relationships. In fact, aside from family members, most people may never find a true career mentor.

There are many examples, including in my personal experience, of mentors who do not hold higher rank or authority on an organization chart. You can tell if you have a true mentor by asking yourself a few questions. *Is this someone I can call at any hour? Is this someone who would do me a favor, big or small, almost every time I ask? Is this someone who will reach out to me just to see how I'm doing or give me a kick in the pants? Do they really know me as a person, and always have my best interests in mind?* We might be lucky enough to count our parents as mentors so we can answer "yes" to these questions. Mentors provide you with the candor (sometimes brutal) that you need, or a stern lecture or a shoulder to cry on. In the workplace, finding someone who really knows you, believes in your potential, and provides support is beyond valuable.

I first met one of my mentors over dinner at a commuter train stop. It was the only place he could meet. From our first interaction, we clicked. I could tell he liked me as a person and wanted to understand what made me tick. The meeting was scheduled for an hour, but we talked until the restaurant closed and the last train was about to depart. Like a successful first date, we had bonded somehow, and the relationship flourished.

About two years later, I was in need of a speaker for a staff meeting in a remote location, to present on improving results and building teams. My mentor happened to call about an exciting technology he had discovered, and I mentioned my meeting. He asked, "What are the dates?" then offered to fly in—at his own expense. My mentor was a highly sought after and highly paid speaker for business groups across the country, yet he came to my tiny team meeting on his own dime because he cared.

Another time, he spotted me in the audience of a speech he was giving, shot across the room and grabbed my arm, saying "Let's get out of here and talk." We spent thirty minutes talking about my family and personal issues, and he ended up starting his speech late. He was *that* interested in how I was doing.

Regardless of workload or schedule constraints, every mentor has always taken time for my issues. In addition to advice and counsel, on occasion they will warn me about landmines or assassins (defined in the next section) they are aware of. Most importantly, they let me know when it is time to change my direction or behavior.

As with fans, beware of false mentors—people who want the credit only when you are succeeding. Unless someone is willing to stand by you when your stock isn't peaking, they are not mentors. One former boss, who moved me through a few different roles, was someone I began to see as a mentor. However, I discovered over time that he was discouraging his peers from promoting me, a fact they shared with me behind closed doors. I was misreading his signals as mentoring when I was simply a valuable asset whom he selfishly tried to keep from leaving.

In another instance, I met my manager for a mentoring beverage and feedback. I needed some help navigating a difficult negotiation. "Don't worry, you have me!" was his reassuring message. Unfortunately, I subsequently discovered he was completely self-absorbed by personal preservation, rendering him incapable of providing any true mentoring feedback. Over time, my colleagues had nicknamed him Benjamin, because he was the antithesis of Benjamin Franklin, who said, "If we don't hang together, we most assuredly will all hang separately."

Real mentors take time to impart real wisdom during coachable moments. They help you decide if you should move to Singapore or open a sports bar in Cincinnati. While most of us have to rely on our fans and the kindness of strangers at most crossroads in our career, being lucky enough to have a business mentor can make all the difference.

In addition to seeking out mentors, aspire to be a mentor yourself. Having a positive impact on someone else's career is extremely rewarding, and the perfect way to pay it forward.

The Assassins

As rare and real as a mentor is The Assassin. Especially as you increase your profile and your following, there may be a few people in your career who actively plot your professional demise. Or you may just get caught as collateral damage in other people's conflicts.

In one instance, which I will return to in a later chapter, a coworker's manager told him as he prepared to move to another company, "I'm glad you are leaving. I will never admit it outside of this room, but I'm sorry you found another job because I was looking forward to firing you." I myself was once told by a colleague, "If I were you, I would start looking outside this company. I'm here, so we don't need you around anymore." While you almost have to admire their candor, knowing there is someone actively trying to push you out never is pleasant.

Here's one of my favorite anecdotes. A member of the company legal team was furious at my colleague and I for trying to reduce fees with an outside law firm. On a conference room speaker phone, he loudly and clearly let us know how and when he was going to get us fired. Because we were well supported by others, he never fulfilled his promise. Afterward, we joked that if our defenders were to ever leave the company, we would be fired within days. But there was probably some truth to that statement.

As with mentors, this relationship is highly personal. During your career, you certainly want to avoid working with or for anyone who puts a target on your back. It is also best to never let your working relationships get to the point where you feel this way about another employee. While there are winners and losers in the normal course of business life, there is no reason to waste energy creating or maintaining enemies.

How to Know Who's Who

These five kinds of relationships are just facts of life. Your goal is to shape the distribution curve in your favor, building the largest possible positive following and minimizing negative relationships. While most may see you indifferently, your goal is to move as many people as possible into becoming your fans. It's always a risk to get to know people and try to become their fans as well. But the risk is worth taking to avoid being invisible or inconsequential. And, as I learned from my fishing poles and golf clubs, be open to letting people see what is in your trunk.

Businesses do not typically reward the bland or the indifferent. Of course, having no filter or inhibitions isn't good practice or common sense either. Once, a national broadcaster said on air that Hall of Fame football quarterback Roger Staubach "ran like a sissy." I remember hearing that with shock; unsurprisingly, I can't remember ever hearing that announcer on a broadcast again. I'm sure even his supportive coworkers and management realized after that single ill-conceived comment, that he had crossed a line and could never recover.

One former manager actually stated his goal was to not have anyone be indifferent about him. "I want colleagues to either like me or hate me because that's how I know I'm at least getting a response and making an impact. Hopefully more people than not up the food chain will like what I do and how I do it."

Challenge yourself to minimize your feelings of disinclination toward others. You should aspire to be a fan of or mentor to as many as you can. If you have negative impressions of others, at least check your facts and personal biases. Unlike your personal life, your organization is paying you to work as a team, and sometimes that means swallowing pride or partnering with people you would rather not. While there are some people who should never work together, almost everyone can weather short-term conflicts for the good of a desired outcome.

If you want to know how a boss or coworker feels about you, spend time with their spouse, significant other, or their children. Even better, have *your* spouse meet them. People you work with are very good at projecting images, but they are usually unfiltered away from the office. One day, the wife of one of my employees stopped by the office unexpectedly. None of us on the team had ever met her before, so we all stopped by to say hello. Suffice it to say that after she departed, all of us were keenly aware of how that employee really felt about each of us, and the company in general. How family members interact with you, and you with them, will speak volumes about the status of a relationship.

Chapter 5: Identifying Various Fish in the Pond

While it is impossible to list all the different characters you will meet on your journey within a company, there are a few noteworthy types to watch out for. The following are usually found in larger organizations.

Waiters

Not servers in restaurants, but folks in an organization who fill a specific task only at certain times. In other words, the person with a very specific skill or expertise who is only needed sporadically. Usually, their skill is very hard to source and even more difficult to cross-train others in. They can be found at every level of the organization, from the assembly line worker with a narrow but critical quality control link, to the specialty lawyer.

If the waiter does not have strong organizational backing, you rarely see them out in the open. They prefer to hunker down in offices or be away from the plant for long periods. Often, while they are "waiting" to execute their tasks, they fill their hours with amusement, and this downtime can be a drain on productivity as they try to draw others into their free time.

Sycophants

Also known as toadies or lackies. If you have ever watched *A Christmas Story* around the holidays—the classic tale of one boy's quest for a Red Rider BB gun—you'll be familiar with this example. Grover Dill is the toadie of the town bully, Scott Farkus. Grover is always at Scott's side, supporting his efforts to terrorize the neighborhood. His presence emboldens Scott, giving him a trusty sidekick to laugh at all his jokes and back his actions. While most organizations have their share of sycophants and bosses who love them, it is very dangerous when the role of toadie becomes a person's core competence.

Amazingly, this group rarely misses a beat when the object of their affection leaves—they will quickly attach themselves to another source to feed on. These folks see the world very much like the main character of *A Christmas Story*, comprised of "bullies, toadies, or one of the nameless rabble of victims."

Make every effort to avoid the toadie, as anything you say or do in their presence can and will be used against you if it serves their agenda or their protectors. If a supervisor tries to mold you into being his personal toadie, carefully consider if that is road you want to travel. It is very hard to reverse course once you do.

Passive Aggressive

These are the folks who rarely speak up in meetings about ideas or conflicts but are quick to expound after the fact. If they are given a task they disagree with, they will outwardly comply but procrastinate. And they are always in the shadows trying to bring colleagues on board with their personal agendas.

Politicians

This bunch is always thinking months or years ahead to their next role. They compete daily for points and see the workplace as competition for the next job. They are keenly attuned to daily power struggles and are up to speed on all the latest dirt. They long to be invited to and noticed at the "right" meetings, and always have to meet the "right" people. They manage strongly upward, but not necessarily in a blatantly sycophant capacity. They jockey for the best parking spots and are always nervous that their car or workstation doesn't make them look prestigious enough. If they are in management positions, they drive their teams after initiatives that further their personal goals, but not necessarily those of the business. If their manager is perceived as standing in the way of their promotion or notoriety, they will actively work around them with subversive or insubordinate activity. This group is also usually quite adept at taking credit for the work of others or at attaching their name to their superior's accomplishments.

Cleaners

When something goes wrong, these are the folks who show up and fix the problem. They exist in almost every functional area of a business, and they are on payroll primarily to clean up any mess. This is the damage control unit, often waiting until such an issue occurs. Check out Harvey Keitel playing the cleaner role in the movie *Pulp Fiction* for a great, albeit extreme, example of this position in action.

Walking Dead

This is an entitled group who, if they were to leave the company tomorrow, would go unnoticed. There would be no need to transfer their duties to others because they don't really have any. They may have received their jobs via nepotism, or they hold a political chip that keeps leaders in fear of repercussions should they leave. It's also possible that their job scope just migrated to others over time and management just hasn't cared enough to notice. They mark their calendars for vacations, retirement, or number of sick days remaining. These folks can kill morale at any business, especially if leadership espouses cost reductions while enabling their dead weight. Like waiters, these folks rarely expose themselves to opportunities for real work, always claiming to be "too busy" doing "stuff."

Mercenaries

For this group, words like "loyalty" and "long term" are not part of the equation. Some people in this tribe are not even aware of playing the part, but find out when they are summarily dismissed as soon as their task is completed. They usually possess a strong work ethic but ultimately are financially driven, willing to complete any mission for a price. If a similar position opens up at another firm for more money, they will quit and pursue it without remorse. They do not generate a fan base because most of the organization can sense they are merely soldiers of fortune.

Traffic Reporters

These folks just tell you bad news but offer no solutions. We have all heard them on our morning commutes: "It's backed up on Interstate 5 for two miles, things are stop and go on the 15, and they are still cleaning up after an accident on the 35 with two lanes shut down. Now back to the music!" This group believes that merely exposing a problem is value added.

Fall Guys

The higher the stakes for any initiative, the greater the need to find someone to play the scapegoat if the desired outcome is not achieved. Many careers have been shut down for being on a team that needs to assign blame for a collective shortcoming. In one previous job, the company culture was so wired for this concept that we would actually wonder who would play this role next: "Who will be Lee Majors this time?" (Lee Majors once starred in a television show called *The Fall Guy*.)

The Secretary

(aka Administrative Assistant, Executive Admin, or Admin) While there are clear examples where this function is required, like CEO support where the phone is literally ringing every minute, or a doctor's office where there has to be a management of constant traffic, the concept is dying out. The secretaries referred to here are those whose only purpose is to serve as eyes and ears for their bosses, a status symbol, or a buffer from unwanted interactions. They serve as waiters until one of those three skills are necessary, and often fill the remaining hours running personal errands for their boss or his family.

Like the sick day, the need for a personal assistant has become somewhat outdated. Prior to the ubiquity of the internet, distributed workforces, and instantaneous communication, this position was invaluable, and as previously noted, remains necessary for certain environments. Yet, there really isn't a need for someone to knock on a door and say, "your two o'clock has just arrived," if the manager only has three daily meetings. Because technology advances have made it possible for most to do for themselves what was once required of an administrative assistant, this type usually is first on the expendable list if a downsizing occurs.

The business world is full of many more characters like those just described, and you no doubt have more than a few other favorites of your own. While they are for the most part generalizations, the reality is that all employees can take on some of these characteristics at various points in their career. Be wary of the labels other people may put on you and be sure your reputation in the company is that of a productive and value-added employee.

Chapter 6: If You Can't Be Successful Here

Ultimately everyone is expendable, at times without cause or notice. The media gives weekly examples of CEOs who abruptly leave without their former companies missing a beat. Companies can lay off thousands and the enterprise continues rolling along. Charles de Gaulle once said it best: "The cemeteries of the world are filled with indispensable men." People are only as indispensable as their severance packages, so never delude yourself that your company won't be able to thrive without you. Always prepare for and stay open to your next job. But remember the adage, *if you want to make God laugh, tell him your plans.* Often the best way to prepare for the next role is to hit home runs in your current one.

One of the hardest things to do is to admit when the game is over for you. So, you must keep your radar on and watch for subtle changes in those around you. If you have a feeling that things are starting to go south, trust it. Reach out to others about those feelings, starting with those who know you best. Mentors can pick up on certain cues you may miss or validate your impressions. A friend of mine was summoned to meeting about a business merger. He reflects, "In hindsight, it was easy to see what was happening. Those who knew they would stay had confident or smug demeanors, while their counterparts looked stunned and worried. Ultimately, operations were not merged, but for those who were not picked as keepers, we knew it was time to get out of there."

You may suddenly stop being invited to certain meetings or functions. New groups may be formed with you conspicuously absent from the roster. Key discussions may occur without you in the loop. Or there may be even more overt signs. A corporation where I worked relocated to a new city and provided blueprints of the new office to the future landlord, with names already marked on each cubicle or office. It was already decided who would and who would not relocate. In an even clearer example, a colleague recounted a jarring discussion with a friend who told him confidentially that his recruiting firm had just been retained to backfill his job. While most signs may not be that clear, a periodic and realistic self-assessment of your status within the company is always recommended.

In that regard, when you make honest mistakes, tell your management about them immediately. A cover-up is almost always worse than the crime, and often the mistake is never as bad as you think. Sometimes, a fan or mentor may be able to serve as a "cleaner" for you and erase a mistake or two. I recall a situation where one senior executive had just made a serious mistake with a contract negotiation in Asia, costing the company over $10 million. Those of us who were aware of it immediately predicted that he would be gone. Instead, I later sat in amazement at meeting with some of his colleagues and his boss as they joked about it. The CEO decided to treat this as a coachable moment. The executive had built up enough credibility, or perhaps had enough of a following, that he could recover from the incident.

When relationships or performance breaks down, it is imperative that you have tools or resources available to deal with it. If your organization includes a Human Resources department, you need to leverage it to the greatest extent you can. Asking for help is hard to do, but that is why HR exists. If your situation is repairable, quickly perform all the action items required to do so.

Chapter 7: Outside of Work

Work is what you do, not who you are. But who you are matters at work.

Don't think that your role ends when you leave the office. A common mistake is to think that people are not assessing you away from the workplace. The earlier example where my boss took stock of the contents of my trunk is a great example.

I remember the day when NBA star Kobe Bryant became an unwitting role model for me. It was January 22, 2007—a bright, sunny Sunday in California. My wife and I arrived at early services at our church. We tucked into the second-to-last row, and I was looking forward to spending the next hour in quiet reflection. About a minute after the service began, I heard someone enter the seat behind us. A quick backward glance revealed that it was Mr. Bryant.

I remember thinking to myself that it was nice for a couple of reasons. First, that he cared enough about his faith to practice it at the crack of dawn during the peak of his busy career. But second, that he cared enough to enter at the last minute so as not be a distraction. One of my favorite parts of our service is the sign of peace, a moment when you say to those around you, "Peace be with you," or just extend a handshake or a warm smile. I turned and shook Kobe's hand and we exchanged smiles. After the service, he slipped away as quietly and seamlessly as he had arrived, with no fanfare.

Later that day, we watched Kobe score 81 points, the second most in NBA history. But I remember the exact date for only one reason. To this day, when that 81-point game is mentioned, I only think about how Kobe spent that early morning. Of all the things he could have done with his time that day, he started it with his faith. I also think about what a good example he was setting as a member of the Laker organization and brand.

You never know who may be watching what you do outside of work. This fact can affect your job, and not always favorably. Once, while flying off to vacation, I noticed a guy who looked vaguely familiar. He wore a suit and was acting very "important"–always put out when someone passes them to use the bathroom or talking loudly on their phone so onlookers can tell they are doing important stuff. Later, as we all shuffled off the plane, the woman sitting next to him headed back a few rows to get her overhead bag. The man audibly grumbled, "You've got to be shitting me," and begrudgingly let her by. Once she retrieved the bag, she tried to retrieve her purse from her seat, which the guy was blocking. He refused to let her reach for her purse and said, "You can wait." She politely asked him to pass her the purse. He replied, "You should have thought of that before you got up," and proceeded to get on his phone. I strained forward to grab the woman's purse and hand it to her. By this time, about a dozen people were watching this scene unfold with disgust and one lady muttered, "What an asshole!"

Then, I noticed the guy's computer case bore *my* company's logo, and I was embarrassed. I made it a point to find out who he was, and then I called his boss. After hearing about the incident, his manager was mortified, but also admitted that this guy had a reputation for being abrasive. In the end, the guy was shocked and embarrassed when his boss and I sat him down and explained how employees are supposed to act at work *and* in public, especially when they are displaying the company logo on their belongings.

When given a choice, be kind. Find a time and place for objective and productive feedback, without disparaging your fellow employees' perceived inadequacies. It is impossible to know what connections people may have in or out of work, and your view of them may vary greatly from others. A colleague learned this the hard way during a staffing review meeting with the CEO, after he had been on a job for only a few months. The CEO randomly asked about Gary, one of the engineers on a project. Now, Gary was known to be a loose cannon with a poor work ethic, who drank the expensive scotch in his desk out of his coffee cup when he was having a bad day. My colleague had been waiting for an opportunity to expose him as a bad employee. He said, "Gary is a total screw-up, and my initial take on him is that he should be fired immediately." My friend describes the long silence that followed, and a feeling that the air had been sucked out of the room. You see, my friend was totally unaware that the CEO and Gary exercised together at 5:00 a.m. every day and had done so for the past five years. He also was unaware that Gary had built a personal relationship with the CEO over that time, which included their wives and children befriending each other. The CEO exploded and the meeting turned into an inquisition of my friend's performance, not Gary's.

While everything my colleague had said was true, he had not seen the blind spot, and his career was irreparably harmed. The lesson is that you must always be on guard about your comments regarding coworkers, bosses, or subordinates, even in seemingly safe situations. You never know how people may interact outside the office or factory.

Chapter 8: Difficult Working Relationships

When you find yourself working for and with people you find difficult, start by truly defining the term "difficult." For example, if your supervisor pushes you to improve and to help the company progress, even into uncomfortable territory, this doesn't make them a difficult person—it actually makes them a great boss. Difficult doesn't mean a less-than stellar bedside manner, nor is it always the cause of conflict. There are already well-documented ways to handle those issues. By *difficult*, I mean someone whose malice or ignorance is hurting you and/or the company—and you have evidence of their harmful words or actions.

In a prior job, I recounted to a trusted colleague every bad decision, conflict, and indignity inflicted on me by a difficult manager. My friend stopped me and said, "Repeat this after me. *I am aware of the part that I play in the creation and maintenance of those situations that victimize me.* Are you sure there was no way to change any of the things you just described?"

At first, I was indignant. But I thought through a few examples and found that he was right. I was playing a key role in all of the situations. Ultimately, I realized I was guilty of a combination of passive aggressive responses, avoidance, or submissive tolerance. The simple truth was that much of my stress was self-imposed, and most of the time I could make a choice to directly address the problems with the other person.

While it may seem much easier to avoid confrontation, the opposite is true. Even if your personality is predisposed to fleeing conflict, facing uncomfortable work situations quickly and head-on is almost always the correct response.

I'll offer a few illustrations. A few weeks into a new position, my boss asked me to bring some data to a meeting with the division president. When I arrived, I noticed my predecessor in the meeting as well. At the end, I asked my boss why my predecessor was there. "Oh, he once had provided some of this analysis, so I just invited him as well." I was shocked and went on the offensive. "Don't you think as the new person who will now get you the data, it would have been important for me to be in that meeting as well? I have only been here a few weeks, but maybe you feel you made a bad decision with me? The optics of that meeting seem to be that you don't value my input and wish you still had him in the role."

My boss apologized and told me all was fine. But he was refusing to address the real issue. I let it go and tried to put it out of my mind. I thought I had done all I could. The scenario repeated itself a few weeks later, but I let it go again, against my better instincts. A few months later at my annual performance review, my boss brought up that initial meeting again. "You know what? You were right. I should have addressed the issue then, but I thought it would correct itself over time. Your colleague is like a warm blanket for me and I continue to use him as a crutch rather than shift the responsibility to you. It's all on me. But I have now created a problem for both of us."

I left the meeting deflated and angry with myself for not insisting months ago that we work through the problem. I should have reached out to others for help as well. Just calling him on it once was never going to create the needed change, and not addressing a bad dynamic only hurt me in the end. We ultimately worked out the issue but lost a lot of productive time by playing the roles of assailant and victim. Recognizing your own role in difficult relationships is the first step in fixing the dynamic.

Sometimes, nothing you do will work. On one particularly long flight I shared with a confidant, I was going on about how challenging my current boss was, and all the things I was doing to address the situation head-on.

My mentor turned to me and said, "Over the years, you may work for some who are rich, some who are mean-spirited, and some who unfortunately are mentally ill. If your boss has any one or two of these characteristics, they can still be valuable to an organization; even a good leader. If you learn that they have all three, run as fast as you can." That was his way of letting me know that he thought my boss fit the description, and that no matter what I did, this person was never going to change.

Chapter 9: Hiring and Firing

Three vital skills you'll need as you gain more responsibility are how to get hired, how to hire people, and how to fire people. Here are some thoughts on addressing your skills in these areas.

Being Interviewed

Once you have been on both sides of the table a few times, you will discover that not many folks are good at being interviewed or interviewing others. Ultimately, candidates and employers are deciding whether to start a lasting relationship and learning as much about each other as possible in a condensed period of time. Focusing on the attributes for success is all that matters.

As a candidate, the obvious basics are: be on time and be prepared to sell yourself. Being prepared includes being focused on every aspect of the interactions you will have. Pay attention to unspoken messages and the interview process itself. For example, if an interviewer unapologetically arrives late or is preoccupied with other matters, that can indicate that your future position isn't vital or that they are already unimpressed with your viability as a candidate. You may be subjected to a lazy interviewer who hasn't even looked at your resume, and so you spend the entire interview rehashing your background. This is, unfortunately, a common phenomenon.

That being said, a bad interviewer does not necessarily dislike you. One of my favorite interviews lasted only 10 minutes. I was sure the manager was giving me the brush off when he abruptly ended the meeting after only two questions; however, I received an offer within the hour. Later, I asked him about the exchange. "I make up my mind quickly and trust my first impression. Plus, I did my homework on your background, and I followed up with other people to validate my judgement."

In addition to selling your personality, your challenge is to turn these discussions into something more than a walkthrough of your historical work stops. You need to craft every response to demonstrate your fit with the job. Make sure that you tailor every answer into an example of one or more of their desired employee attributes. Expect to be thrown off your game a few times and prepare for it.

Civility and etiquette have unfortunately disappeared from the hiring process. Today, when you apply for a job, it is rare to even receive a courtesy confirmation of receipt of your resume and cover letter. In most cases, silence is the new "no thank you." This unfortunately provides a candidate no feedback on what the cause for rejection may be.

When you're a candidate for a job, remember that at least one, or perhaps a few of the people you speak with, will not think you are the right person. As mentioned earlier, aspire to leave every person with a strong opinion about you, whether positive or negative. No one should be indifferent about you after an interview.

After you receive an offer, try to get as much feedback as possible on any concerns people may have had about you or something you said. If someone came away with a negative first impression, it is best to discover that immediately. Due to potential liability, if you do not get an offer for a job, companies will rarely, if ever, give you any feedback on why that was the case. This is an unfortunate reality but try to objectively assess your performance during the process. If you are aware of who ultimately received the opportunity, you may discover what experiences or attributes made them more attractive.

Finally, never try to be an actor when interviewing. Stay authentic. Trying to portray anything but yourself to a company is a disservice to both parties and may unwittingly cost you the job.

Interviewing Others

A great deal of work must be done before a candidate ever arrives at the door. If the role is important, be prepared and be respectful of everyone's time. Be clear about what you want to learn during the interview that you can't learn from the candidate's resume. Even if you are not the primary decision-maker in the process, consider what you can discover that will help that individual make up her mind.

Assuming they landed the interview because their resume is strong or they are up for a promotion, the best use of everyone's time is to assess personal attributes and possible fit with the team. One former manager had a great way of determining whether to hire someone. "Imagine this person will be part of your team for the rest of your career. Do you believe that strongly in them?" This approach keeps you focused on maximizing your learning during the interview.

It's true that most people make up their mind about someone within the first few minutes, so always minimize an initial encounter to thirty minutes or less. Never waste your valuable time on a "rubber stamp" interview that is just going through the motions on a candidate whose fate is already decided.

Never be a lazy or arrogant interviewer. Star candidates with multiple opportunities will see through "Take me through your resume" and know that you never took the time to learn about them. Also, you can't allow a candidate to use up interview time delivering a scripted manifesto or commercial for themselves. Exchanges that focus specifically on gauging the six attributes of the person (see Chapter 1) are all that matter. Save any small talk for after the discussion.

I have found that you learn most about a candidate (and therefore expedite your decision), by asking about their personal perspectives and the unexpected. Lowering a candidate's guard and getting them off their prepared script will gain you the most information.

The following list is a sample of go-to interview questions I have used to expose confidence level and ability to think and react quickly. These questions also lead to great follow-ups.

1. Do you have a nickname? How did you get it?
2. What is one thing you must do every day, without which your day will be bad?
3. What did you dream about becoming when you a kid?
4. What was the most memorable or significant gift you ever received?
5. What is your biggest motivator? What gives the most meaning to your life?
6. Tell me about a time at work when your boss or coworkers were the angry with you. Explain why and how you repaired the relationships.

7. How did you address the biggest failure in your career to date?

8. What was your most creative or innovative accomplished at work? (could be a project, a solution to a problem, etc.)

9. If money were not an object, what would be your dream job?

10. What is your biggest fear, and how have you tried to overcome it?

11. Outside of family members, tell me about one of your role models or mentors, and how they have influenced you.

12. Where was your last vacation and why did you go there? What did you learn or discover during your travels?

13. What can you bring to our company that will improve our product or service or make our customers happier? (This can be drilled down and tailored to any role. i.e., for finance: How can your skill set influence our earnings or increase cash flow?)

Some companies will give puzzles, problems, or IQ tests, depending on the competencies needed for a role. At the end of the day, you only care about getting the best sense of whether someone possesses all of the necessary attributes for the job.

Don't outsource the interview process or candidate selection. Doing so usually ends with dissatisfaction.

People who don't know your culture will find candidates who will fit a typecast, without real examination of whether they are maximizing the attributes you need. You will only discover people who are a good match by putting personal effort into the process. Plus, major search firms and small staffing agencies live up to the moniker of head hunters. While they provide a pre-screen of resumes they perceive as the top, they may also inadvertently weed out some of the real stars who could be the perfect fit for you. Unlike the hiring company, they have a risk-free environment. If a candidate ultimately becomes a star, they take the credit, but if someone flames out in 30-90 days, they merely blame the hiring manager for picking the wrong horse and will still invoice for their fee.

Also, avoid forced arrangements at all costs. If your boss tells you he is reassigning someone to your team, or a candidate is "strongly suggested" by a senior executive, think twice. While you may gain short term favor from the person who "helped you" staff a position, it is extremely rare that you are getting the best candidate for the job. Remember the importance of fit.

Firing People

When it comes to firing people, baseball uses a softer term, which George Carlin masterfully detailed in a comedy sketch. In business, people get fired. In baseball, people get "designated for assignment." It sounds more like they are sending players on a secret mission for the club, but it really just means they are terminating their services.

There is nothing worse in business than getting the axe. Having to fire someone is only slightly less distasteful. No one trains you for it, and there are no perfect ways to do it. When you are the person across the desk, the employee will often hold you personally responsible, no matter how well deserved the termination. Knowing the unpleasant reality of terminating others prevents many people from taking on managerial responsibility.

Being able to let someone go is a competence, and not everyone has it. Many people, even managers of large groups, are incapable of saying those words to another person. One colleague was only comfortable firing someone over the phone, and the HR department unfortunately allowed him to use this practice. He would have the IT and HR departments shut off their computer access and deactivate their key cards while he was on the phone with them. No one should ever be fired by phone or email or text. People deserve the respect of a candid and face-to-face ending to their jobs.

Sometimes it is just necessary to "weed the garden," as one of my former bosses put it. Companies can become over-staffed as business needs shift. Some organizations still use the "rank and yank" process to force this pruning exercise, while others are less disciplined but inevitably achieve the same result over time.

To determine if a group has exceeded its needed capacity, ask employees regularly to describe the top three tasks they are working on. If they list items that don't fill up a full work week, it could be a bad sign. Once, I walked into a colleague's office and noticed a lot of inappropriate art glamorizing a drug lifestyle, and that the centerpiece of his desk was a checkerboard with shot glass pieces. I asked, "What are the top three things you are working on these days?" His response was, "Whatever you need me to do." He literally had nothing of value for the business on his plate.

Good and Bad Reasons to Fire Someone

Obviously, if a company goes out of business, the workforce will need to depart. Downsizing, either due to cost cutting or redundancies in staffing, is also a valid reason. Any violation of law or behavior counter to company core values are also grounds for dismissal. Finally, any employee who does not have one or more of the required employee attributes might be let go at any time.

However, personal bias with no required effort to improve a relationship is not a sufficient reason to let someone go. Management may use the excuse of a "bad fit" to cover up the motives of an assassin. This is where Human Resources must provide protection. Sometimes new managers want to bring in their own team, rather than work with assets in place, but this is never a good reason for termination either. There must be some objective evidence that a person lacks one or more of the variables need to be successful.

If you are in the unfortunate position of having to terminate someone, remember that if given a choice between a quick bullet to the head or five shots to the body and a slow bleed out, you would be hard pressed to find anyone to take option number two. If you must fire someone, do it quickly and with as much empathy as possible. If the discussion lasts more than five minutes, it has gone on too long.

If you are the one who is let go, keep in mind that most cases are not personal. Denial, isolation, anger, bargaining, depression, and ultimate acceptance can all be part of the unpleasant process. If it does happen to you, learn from the experience. For example, if there was a downsizing, objectively assess why were you on the list to depart and not others. If it was due to a personal deficiency, improve in that area for your next opportunity. Rarely will employers go into detail about why or want to have a protracted dialogue with you about it. As the saying goes, if you are going through hell, keep going. Reach out to the people both in and out of the organization who may be able to help you. If you are suddenly designated for assignment, start your comeback as soon as possible. Don't wallow. Be unstoppable.

Chapter 10: Managing vs. Leading

Management is different from Leadership. Here are some snack-sized thoughts about both.

Management

If you are a manager or aspire to become one, here are some tips for success. A twist on an old expression says, *gather all the fruit on the ground before even getting to the low hanging stuff.*

First, managing is different from leadership. Managers are not necessarily leaders. Think of managing similarly to parenting or coaching. Treat people who work for you the way they *need* to be treated in order to grow and for the company to prosper. There is no "golden rule" (treat people the way you would want to be) or "platinum rule" (treat people the way they want to be) in parenting, and the same is true in managing. Treat everyone on your team equally, but never manage them all the same way. Some people are more motivated and productive when pushed, others are self-directed and would be hindered by micromanagement, especially if already giving their best. Learn what motivates each person and develop them individually. Gaining a team's trust and respect and getting them to perform at their highest level are all that matter. If you are only looking to be liked, management may not be for you.

Remember to be authentic. Trying to be someone else or acting the way you believe a manager should is a recipe for failure. Direct reports need to build up credibility with you, and you with them. Emulate the practices of good managers but remain true to yourself in the process.

Getting to know your team personally is the best way to begin building credibility. The fastest way to lose it is by exuding that you only see them as tools to accomplish work. Give the team the credit for victories and take personal blame for shortfalls.

Vin Scully, the legendary sports broadcaster once quipped, "Statistics get used much like a drunk uses a lamppost: for support, not illumination." Unfortunately, many managers view employees the same way. Good employees want to illuminate as well as support. Managers should ask themselves often what their team is teaching them. Because if you are not learning anything from your team, it's a safe bet that you are not managing effectively.

With all the knowledge and wisdom available from countless sources, there is no excuse for a manager not to have a roadmap for almost any issue. You'll even find great tools from authors who have never been managers. Find what resonates with you among the dogma or misguided information out there. Here are just two examples that have helped me to become a better manager and employee.

In *Winning Every Day*, former football coach Lou Holtz identifies three questions to assess whether personal or business relationships are out of alignment.

1. Do I trust this person (and have I given them a reason to trust me)?
2. Is this person committed to excellence (and have I shown them my commitment to excellence)?
3. Does this person care about me or my goals (and have I shown them I care)?

Every *no* exposes a problem and possible solution, and if left unaddressed, the relationship won't likely survive. Every single workplace relationship has proven this to be true in my experience, whether managerial, lateral, or upward. Note that these questions are not about personalities, likes, dislikes, or politics. For every personal or team issue you may encounter as a manager, asking these questions is a good way to find common ground.

When a close friend was recently *designated for assignment* (outlined earlier in this guide) his boss said during the severance discussion, "I never really liked you from the first time we met. I can't really explain it other than to just admit that we never really hit it off." Because he was hearing this feedback for the first time on the day he was let go, my friend was bewildered. He immediately assumed that his boss was assassinating him without cause.

While it's possible that this was a mean-spirited parting shot, I was reminded of Holtz's three questions. I told my buddy that what he probably meant to communicate was, "I never really trusted you." Likely, my friend had never trusted his boss either, and neither had made the effort to address the relationship, which had grown unsustainable. My explanation seemed to make him feel better and gave him a way to connect the dots to something actionable for his future. He could learn from this problem of fit, rather than just leave thinking he had been terminated for personal bias.

As I reflect on every employee I have let go (mostly excluding downsizing or cost cutting necessities), a "no" answer to at least one of Holtz's questions was the root cause. Even when cost cutting was the reason, the tie breaker for people who were kept has usually been "yes" answers to the questions.

Another book I find valuable is *Execution* by Larry Bossidy and Ram Charan. Before beginning any new management position with a group, I leaf through that book to remind myself of the processes needed to get things done. The prerequisites to being able to execute are

1) "social software" mechanisms to reinforce company culture; 2) reality and candor at the heart of all decisions; and 3) having the right people in the right place doing the right thing. Consider whether your current organization is dysfunctional, and it's a safe bet you'll notice it's missing at least one prerequisite. In those cases, even small initiatives or short-term projects become impossible to accomplish.

Proving my point, years ago my CEO held an emergency team meeting to generate ideas to improve results. The board was seeking to generate another $10-$20 million of margin out of our operations. Many of us believed that we could get most, if not all of the needed results out of our major markets, and so I volunteered to work on it. The CEO was skeptical, but he told me to work directly with the managers leading those markets and draw a path to success. We did thorough market studies and identified ways to cut $10 million of expense without adversely impacting the company. We also brainstormed actionable ways to improve revenue.

The CEO was surprised by how much low-hanging fruit we had found, and he promised to let the board know our findings. I later came to discover from one of the managers I was set to work with that the CEO actually never intended to share any of the ideas, much less execute the plan. When confronted, the CEO confirmed his intentions. "I really disagree with the cuts, and I am not convinced we should make any pricing changes. I will tell the board what I think is appropriate." He ultimately told the board members that there was "no way" to find any additional margin. The culture and social mechanism fostered by this person would not allow even a little progress, or even a surfacing of ideas. If you manage others, there are countless bad management practices to avoid. You may already be familiar with some of the following examples if you have ever worked for an imperfect boss.

- Creating busy work so the team has to stay late, then ordering takeout just so the manager won't have to eat alone.

- Asking employees who are leaving for a colleague's child's birthday party after the work day, "You're coming back later, right?" even though no work remains to be done.

- Undermining their team's authority by announcing in meetings, "If you need a quick answer, call me directly. Don't assume that your manager is going to ask me."

- Locking their office door during business hours and only allowing subordinates to be buzzed in after a pre-screen of their issues, all while touting an open-door policy.

- Berating an employee loudly in their office while the speaker phone is activated so that dozens of other employees can hear. Then, refusing to be accountable for that behavior.

- Favoring a few employees and making others aware of their exclusion. Then, using those special encounters to conduct work that later heighten the dynamic of favoritism and exclusion.
- Insisting on questionable social interaction with their direct reports and rewarding those who comply.
- Hiding in their office all day when headquarters is calling for an immediate answer to a question and having their "secretary" lie about their whereabouts.
- Having someone else on their team fire a direct report because they don't want to deal with it.
- Misusing company resources for personal gain. As an example, having the company pay for their family to accompany them on an extended work trip, only to spend their work time on leisure activities and failing to accomplish the objective of the trip.

The behaviors on this list are only top of mind examples which I witnessed firsthand. There are many more I could recount, and I'm sure you have your own to add. Everyone, except perhaps the offenders, can agree the behaviors are wrong, but they can go unchecked due to position or an enabling culture. If you have managerial responsibility, learn from any prior imperfect bosses and don't emulate their worst practices.

Leadership

Like title inflation, the word *leader* has become synonymous with *manager*. Do not be fooled. There are very few true leaders in any organization. Most employees are hard pressed to identify the good "leaders" in their business, yet almost every person above them on the organizational chart seems to think they are in fact leaders.

Well led organizations share core practices:

1. Most of team has confidence that the folks in charge are doing, will continue to do, the "right" things for the business.
2. Clearly articulated goals and a well-defined critical path exist for the group, with buy-in from the team and repercussions if milestones are not met.
3. Internal and external constituents understand and adhere to a shared culture.

If you are not creating or influencing these practices, you are not really leading. If the people in "leadership positions" at your firm are not driving these practices, neither are they.

In groups that are not well led, we see common patterns, subtler than simply the opposite of the good core practices above. Passing the buck usually indicates a leadership void. People who are captains of industry or even run countries may not have any leadership qualities, but that is not alarming in and of itself. As long as there are people who have directional skills, i.e., they intuitively know a direction that an organization needs to move toward, or outstanding business judgement, that is usually all that is required to successfully run a business. Yet, the irony is that people who are outstanding leaders may be totally devoid of those skills.

Never mistake charisma for leadership. Many people with great interpersonal and negotiation skills may be touted as great leaders while their business goes into bankruptcy. Some people are born leaders, but it is also possible to become a good leader after first learning to be a good *follower.*

Managers have authority from their titles, but leaders garner respect and influence behavior beyond their direct reports. Ask yourself, who, if anyone, views *you* as a leader, and why? Is it your business acumen, character, or do you merely have the adoration and acceptance of sycophants? Leaders attract teams that share their vision, and they influence morale and performance with words and actions. Leaders provide hope, and they make a personal impact. Unlike managers, leaders don't tend to call themselves leaders—they don't have to.

At a meeting near the top floor of a high-rise, the fire alarm sounded before we could even begin. Those running the show were quick to inform us of a leak from the kitchen above and assure us that the alarm would stop in a minute, which it did. As we brought the meeting back to order, we realized that the president of the company was absent, as was her toadie executive right-hand man. They had taken to the stairwell the instant the alarm went off, afraid of a serious situation. The two of them finally made their way back up to the meeting room ten minutes later, but the damage had already been done. Whispers about her "leadership" circulated. Everyone agreed that if she had been that concerned about safety, she should have demanded that everyone evacuate with her.

Conversely, at a different conference with about forty coworkers, champagne arrived unexpectedly. The drinks were to celebrate the team's recent successes and for general recognition of our efforts. The group downed every bottle like prohibition had just ended. Our group leader who had ordered the drinks was noticeably absent. He arrived later and asked if the group enjoyed the surprise. I remember feeling terrible that he hadn't gotten any champagne since he was the one who deserved it most. Later, he went out of his way to handwrite notes to everyone's significant other or spouse, thanking them for their support while we worked 60-80 hours for weeks on end. Most of that team would have run through a wall for him because of all the little ways he showed how much he cared about the group, and us as individuals. Had *he* been in that fire-alarm meeting, he would have been the *last* person to exit after he was sure that the rest of the team was safe.

Final Thoughts

As stated at the outset, the goal of this guidebook is to provide some back-of-the-envelope advice and ideas to navigate the employment world. A secondary objective was to provoke some thought and knock down a few strawmen. Everyone's journey is different, and hopefully your experiences have provided you with volumes of supplemental learning that no single text—much less a handbook—could possibly provide.

After years of coaching fellow workers and seeking coaching from others, this manual represents many, but certainly not all, common themes that arose. Companies are like people, in that everyone is different. Whether in the lunch room or during formal reviews, you will discover most of the unwritten rules of your specific employer over time. Your curiosity, ability to ask questions and listen to the answers, will determine how quickly you obtain that knowledge.

Most company employee manuals or websites don't provide you with a list of questions you should be asking.

It is my hope that this one has given you good questions to consider. The most common mistake that employees make is to stop growing or learning, even as they get promoted. Knowledge truly is power, and your inquisitiveness to learn, discover, and innovate can separate you from the pack.

During a multi-week project years ago, the leader was cynically asked by a team member, "What do you expect to get out of this project?" The leader responded, "Teach me something." That changed the mindset from just another task to *let's discover something*.

Your employer expects great things from you. Good luck and get back to work!

Chapter Summaries

1. Understand what it takes to be a great employee, and work on every aspect of your game to achieve that goal. Realize the detriments of missing any of the attributes.
2. Be well versed in the objectives and reality of your organization. Know when and how those objectives and the culture may change over time.
3. Make positive steps to work on both the tangible and intangible aspects of your job. It is often the subtle things that can trip you up or cloud your decision making.
4. Realize that people are constantly assessing you a person and employee, and that you have the power to change most of those assessments over time.
5. In larger companies, many labels or roles will exist that may not make sense to you. Stay focused on what you are doing and avoid groups that may be detrimental to your growth and development.
6. You are not perfect, and things will not always go well. Develop tools or identify resources to help you when things get off track.
7. What you do outside of work influences how people see you at work.
8. People you work with are not perfect either, but you need to find common ground to work as well as you can with everyone.

9. Learn how to hire and fire people if you want to be a successful manager. Work on skills that will get you hired, and those that will minimize your risk of being let go.

10. If you are or will soon be a manager, understand that leadership is not needed to manage, and management skills are not necessarily required to be a leader.

Works Cited

Bossidy, Larry, et al. *Execution: The Discipline of Getting Things Done.* Currency, 2002.

Holtz, Lou. *Winning Every Day.* Harper Business, 1998.

43983646R00060

Made in the USA
Middletown, DE
01 May 2019